C IS FOR CHICKASAW

ISBN 978-1-935684-19-0

Book and cover design: Aaron K. Long

White Dog Press
c/o Chickasaw Press
PO Box 1548
Ada, Oklahoma 74821
www.chickasawpress.com

IS FOR
CHICKASAW

DEDICATION

For my wife Rachel,
my best friend who always inspires me.
For my children, Layla and Evan,
you are the light so that I can see.

- Wiley Barnes

To God for the opportunity and ability, to Jannason for
her love and the time, and to Andrew, Wyatt, Audrey,
and Arabella–anything is possible!

- Aaron Long

THE ARTWORK

The illustrations in this book were created in a style known as Southeastern Native American Art. Specifically, they reflect the style found on ancient shell engravings from the Mississippian period. Subjects in this style are shown in profile and are represented one dimensionally with highly stylized features. Vibrant color has been added to make them fun and interesting for children. Southeastern Native artists and artisans draw inspiration from the traditions of their ancient ancestors from the Mississippi River valley which is part of the Southeastern Ceremonial Complex.

The objects and art Southeastern artists fashioned then—and create now—echo and affirm the identities of their people.

C
IS FOR
CHICKASAW

BY WILEY BARNES

ILLUSTRATED BY AARON LONG

WHITE DOG PRESS

CHICKASAW

CHIKASHA

A Native American tribe rich in history
Proud, strong, and beautiful people you will want to see

Chickasaws are a Native American tribe. They are an indigenous people of the Southeastern Woodlands. The traditional Chickasaw homeland was in the Southeastern United States. Their territory included parts of Mississippi, Alabama, Tennessee, and Kentucky.

C
IS FOR
CHICKASAW

BY WILEY BARNES
ILLUSTRATED BY AARON LONG

WHITE DOG PRESS

ARROW

OSKI' NAKI'

Flying silently and swiftly through the air
Warriors hunt for food, fish, deer, even bear

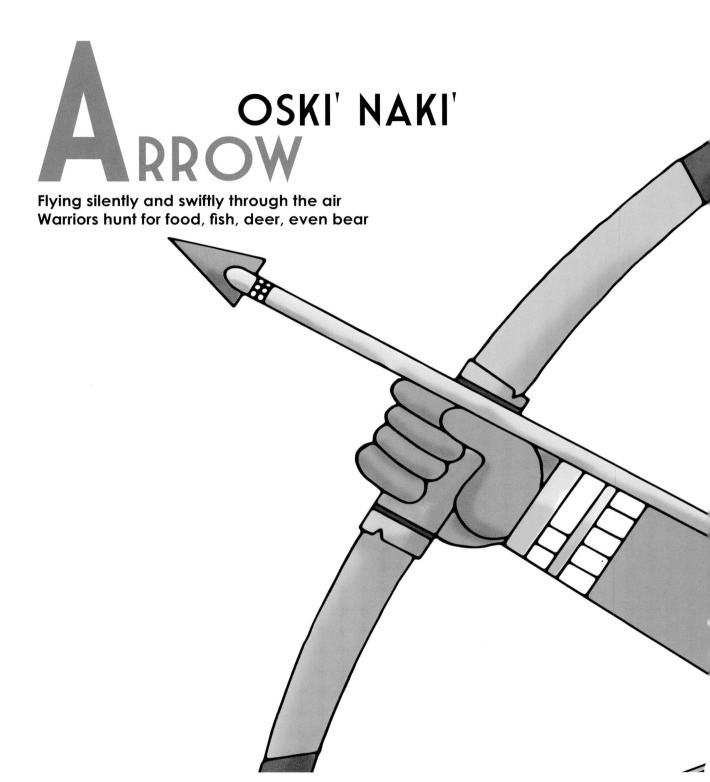

Arrows are used for hunting, fishing, and sport. Chickasaws have used arrows for centuries. The arrowheads are handmade from flint in a process called flint knapping. Flint knapping is shaping the rock by striking it and chipping pieces off. The arrowheads are attached to river cane. Feathers, called fletching, are attached to the river cane to help stabilize the arrow.

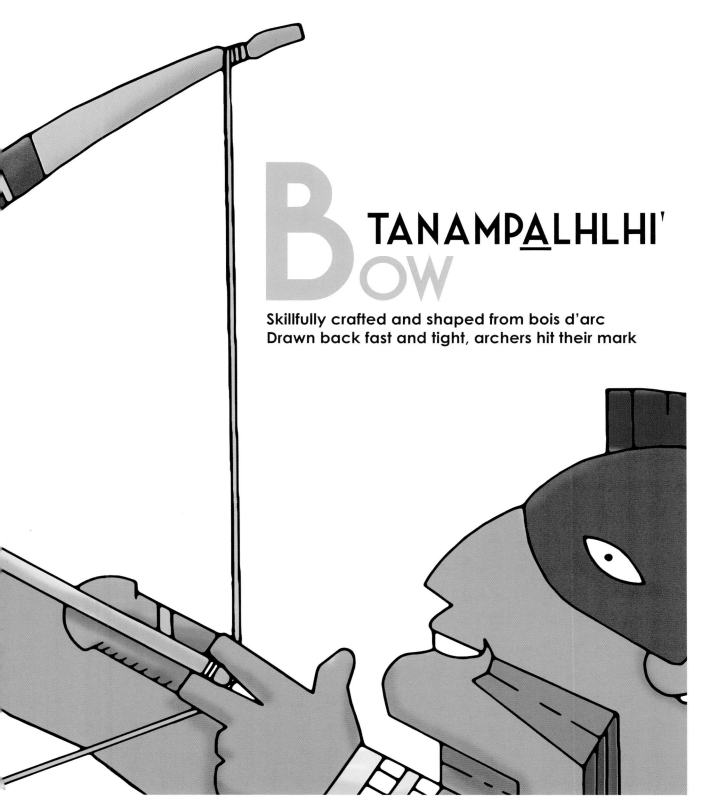

Bow
TANAMP**A**LHLHI'

Skillfully crafted and shaped from bois d'arc
Drawn back fast and tight, archers hit their mark

A bow makes an arrow fly through the air. Before European contact, bows and arrows were the primary choice for protection and hunting. Chickasaws were known for their archery skills. Their bows and arrows were handcrafted from bois d'arc and prized by every hunter in ancestral tribal lands.

Chickasaw

CHIKASHA

A Native American tribe rich in history
Proud, strong, and beautiful people you will want to see

Chickasaws are a Native American tribe. They are an indigenous people of the Southeastern Woodlands. The traditional Chickasaw homeland was in the Southeastern United States. Their territory included parts of Mississippi, Alabama, Tennessee, and Kentucky.

The Chickasaw were forced to move to Indian Territory during the time of Indian Removal in the 1830s. Some tribes call Indian Removal the Trail of Tears. Today, the Chickasaws are a federally recognized tribe known as the Chickasaw Nation. The Chickasaw Nation is now in Oklahoma. The Chickasaw are a proud people with a great history of survival, achievement, and beauty.

DANCE
HILHA'

Rhythmic feet circling around the sacred fire
Listen to the songs, prayers lifted higher

Chickasaws pray and celebrate life with song and dance. Traditional Chickasaw song and dance is called stomp dance and is held during social events. Tribal members of all ages come together to shake shells, sing, and dance counter-clockwise around a sacred fire. Many dances performed today were passed down from ancient times.

ELDER

KAMASSA'

Older members of the tribe are honored and respected
Sharing wisdom and tradition carefully collected

Elders are important older members of the tribe. Chickasaw elders are respected for their knowledge, wisdom, and courage. They play a role in passing along traditions, stories, and culture. Chickasaws always respect and honor their elders.

FOSHI' HISHI'
FEATHER

**Used to honor and decorate
All that are noble, brave, and great**

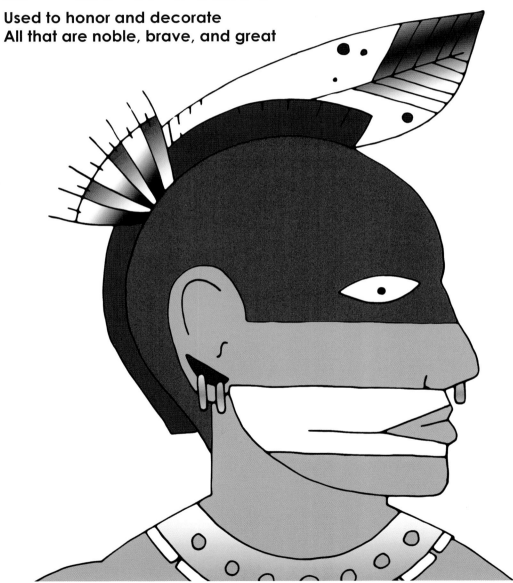

Swan and turkey feathers were attached to capes or wraps and given to the most brave and noble Chickasaw warriors. Eagle feathers were also used for religious, healing, marriage, and naming ceremonies. Feathers have special meaning because they come from birds that fly above in the heavens. Feathers are also used in the making of arrows.

<u>I</u>NAALHPISA'
GOVERNMENT

Chickasaw Nation has a tribal government
Three branches provide successful empowerment

The Chickasaw Nation has a tribal government with its own legislature, police, laws, and services for its citizens. The government has executive, judicial, and legislative branches much like the United States government. The Chickasaw Nation has a constitution and holds elections for government officials who work to enhance the overall quality of life for Chickasaw people.

HELLO
CHOKMA

Chokma is how to say hello and greet
Speak Chickasaw and new friends you will meet

Use Chokma to greet others in Chickasaw. This greeting means, "Hello," or, "Are you well?" You can also say, "Chinchokma? (Are you okay?)." They can answer by saying, "Anchokma!" (I'm good!)."

HATTAK API' HOMMA' IYAAKNI'
INDIAN TERRITORY

The Chickasaws were forced to settle in this new place
The journey was long with many challenges to face

Indian Territory was land set aside by the United States for the forced re-settlement of Native Americans. It was created by the Indian Intercourse Act of 1834. The Chickasaws, and other tribes, were forced to give up their land in the east and move to land in Indian Territory. Later it became part of the state of Oklahoma.

Joy ᎠᎣᎩᏆ AYOKPA

Grandmother, grandfather, mother, father, sister, brother
Family is important, spending time with each other

Families are important to keep traditions and culture alive. Mothers are the center of a Chickasaw family. Family heritage, including which clan someone belongs to, is traced through the mother. Each clan is represented by an animal and has a specific duty like gathering, raising, and hunting for food.

KALI-HOMMA'
KULLIHOMA

A place with tradition where families celebrate
Reuniting with old friends is especially great

Kullihoma is a 1,500-acre Chickasaw tribal reserve. It has deep roots in Chickasaw history and is a favorite gathering place for Chickasaw people. It was once an active stomp ground, school, and community. Visitors to Kullihoma can see examples of traditional houses including a winter house, summer house, council house, and corn crib.

LANOMPA
LANGUAGE

**Learn and speak Chickasaw everyday
You can make sure it is here to stay**

Chikashshanompa' (Chickasaw language) is part of the Muskogean language family. It is a vital part of Chickasaw cultural identity. Today there are fewer than sixty-five fluent speakers of the language. There are classes, books, websites, and mobile apps to give Chickasaws the tools they need to learn this endangered language.

MOCCASINS
SHOLOSH

**Deerskin sewn together makes this native shoe
Protecting feet from thorns and cold weather too**

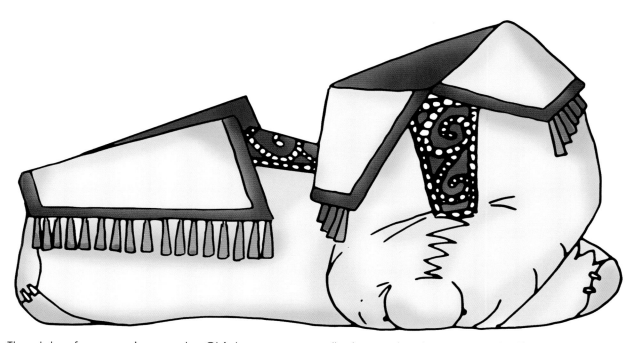

The style of moccasin worn by Chickasaws was called a pucker-toe moccasin. They were made from a single piece of deerskin. The deerskin was sewn from the instep to the toe, and a flap was left around where the foot went in. Chickasaws wore moccasins in cold weather and to protect their feet when they traveled. The rest of the time they went barefoot.

N HOLHCHIFO
NAME

Introduce yourself to someone and ask their name
Speak Chickasaw to friends and they may do the same

Chickasaws say Saholhchifoat and their name to say, "My name is _____."

When someone asks you what your name is you can respond by saying,

"Saholhchifoat _____. (My name is _____.)"

To ask someone their name in Chickasaw, say, "Nanta chiholhchifo? (What is your name?)"

OKLAHOMMA'

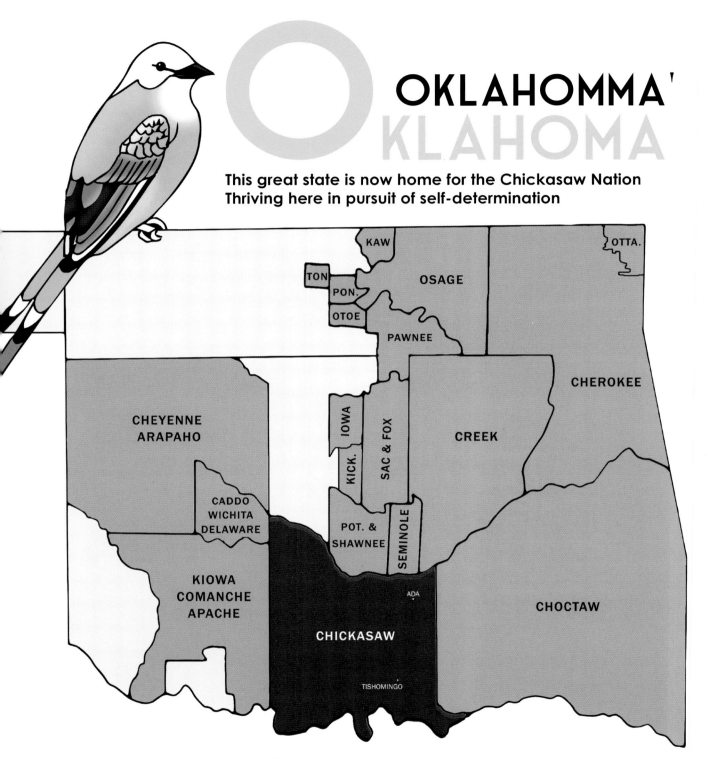

**This great state is now home for the Chickasaw Nation
Thriving here in pursuit of self-determination**

KAW

OTTA.

TON

OSAGE

PON.

OTOE

PAWNEE

CHEROKEE

IOWA

KICK.

SAC & FOX

CREEK

CHEYENNE
ARAPAHO

CADDO
WICHITA
DELAWARE

POT. &
SHAWNEE

SEMINOLE

KIOWA
COMANCHE
APACHE

ADA

CHOCTAW

CHICKASAW

TISHOMINGO

Oklahoma's name comes from the Choctaw words okla, which means people, and humma, which means red. The Chickasaw Nation is located in south-central Oklahoma. It covers thirteen counties. The Chickasaw Nation headquarters is in Ada, Oklahoma. Chickasaw citizens live and work in Oklahoma, as well as all over the United States and around the world.

PISHOFA

TASHPISHOFA

Paddle stirring and steam rising from the big pot
Cooked over fire, this corn and pork dish is served hot

Pishofa is a Chickasaw traditional dish made of cracked corn and pork. It has been important in religious and social activities for hundreds of years. The pishofa ceremony brought a family together to help heal the sick. Today, pishofa is cooked at social events to honor the Chickasaws' cultural traditions.

QUIVER

OSKI' NAKI' AALHTO'

Holds and protects arrows for transport
Sometimes designed for hunting or sport

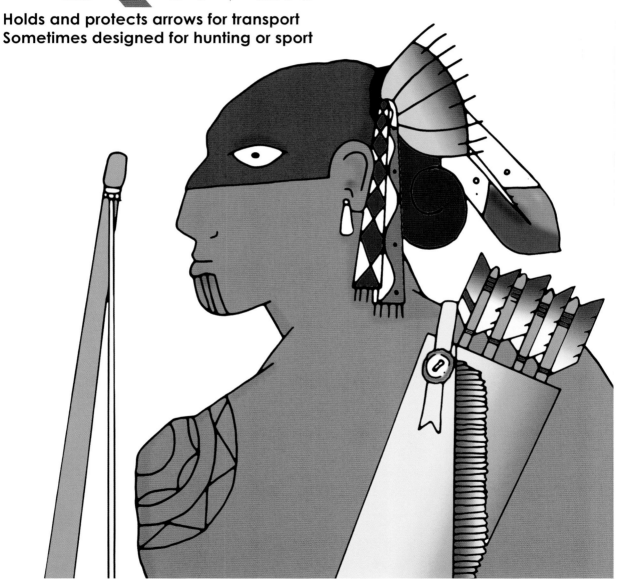

A quiver holds arrows. Chickasaw warriors and hunters used quivers made of deerskin. A quiver could carry and protect several arrows. The quiver on the Great Seal of the Chickasaw Nation has special meaning. It represents the hunting expertise of the Chickasaw warrior, as well as his willingness to defend his people.

R EGALIA
NAAFOKHA

**Bright ribbon shirts and beautiful, long dresses flowing
On special occasions Chickasaws wear this clothing**

Traditional clothing worn for special occasions is called regalia. In the past, Chickasaws made clothing from animal skins or fabric woven from plant fibers. Today, Chickasaw regalia includes ribbon shirts and dresses, finger-woven belts, beaded collars, hair combs, silver gorget neckwear, armbands, and turbans or hats decorated with turkey or eagle feathers.

STICKBALL

KAPOCHCHA' TO'LI'

**Running and throwing the woven ball to score
A tough game called the little brother of war**

Chickasaws have played stickball for hundreds of years. It is played with two wooden sticks and a woven ball. The sticks are used to hold and catch the ball, and players score by hitting the ball on a pole on either side of the field. Long ago, the game was used to train young warriors or settle disputes between tribes, which is why it was called "the little brother of war."

TISHOMINKO

A great warrior, speaker, and leader; wise and strong
Lived to be one hundred, his life was full and long

Tishominko means "*assistant leader.*" He was a well-respected Chickasaw warrior and speaker. His image appears on the Great Seal of the Chickasaw Nation because his life and values represent what it means to be Chickasaw. The city of Tishomingo, Oklahoma, home to the Chickasaw National Capitol building, is named for Tishominko.

UNCONQUERED

IKIMAMBO

**Intrepid warriors and dynamic women
Showing strength and honor, again and again**

Chickasaws are unconquered and unconquerable. They are a proud people that have overcome many obstacles throughout history. Known for their intrepid, or fearless, warriors and dynamic women, the Chickasaw people are confident in a bright future and continued success. They serve one another and teach their children to do the same.

V NANNAWAA'
VEGETABLE

**Corn, beans, and squash are all delicious vegetables grown
Called the Three Sisters, planted together, not alone**

Chickasaws planted corn, beans, and squash together, so they could support and nourish each other. This is called companion planting. The corn is planted in the middle and provides a support for the beans to climb, and the beans provide nitrogen for the soil. The squash provides cover to prevent weeds and help retain moisture.

OFI' TOHBI'

WHITE DOG

This legendary dog was a great scout
Always protecting the tribe on their route

In the Chickasaw's great migration story, the White Dog is the tribe's scout and protector. Long ago, the Chickasaw people decided to look for a new home. Their journey led them to the Mississippi River. They built rafts to cross. One of the rafts came apart, and the White Dog was separated from everyone else. The White Dog was unable to continue the journey.

Xylography is the art of engraving wood. Chickasaws have used items available to them in nature for thousands of years. Wood has been essential for tools, houses, dugout canoes, and bows.

X YLOGRAPHY

TALHLHI

Chipping and chiseling Southeastern designs
The art of carving in wood with shapes and lines

Southeastern Native art is a work in any form inspired by the Southeastern Ceremonial Complex. The Southeastern Ceremonial Complex is a style of art that comes from the region where the Mississippian peoples once lived. It uses certain symbols, subjects, styles, colors, or textures to show details of their lives and environment.

Yarn

Nantanna' Toba'

Lovely belt made by a Chickasaw hand
Finger weaving each individual strand

Yarn is used in the ancient art of finger-weaving. Finger-weaving is the art of weaving items without a loom. Chickasaws use finger-weaving to make straps, garters, belts, and sashes. Yarn is used today, but ancient Chickasaws used woven plant fibers.

ZIGZAG
FOLOTO'WA

**Bright colors and patterns repeated
Extra details make this completed**

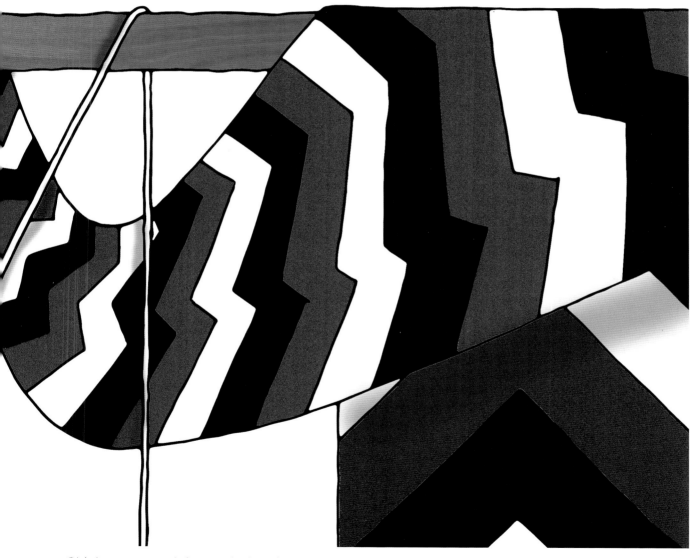

Chickasaws used zigzag designs in art and clothing. Ancient Southeastern tribes, including the Chickasaw, used animal figures to decorate. They also used geometric shapes such as arrows, chevrons, and zigzags. Beads and feathers were often used for decoration as well.

GLOSSARY

ENGLISH WORD	CHICKASAW	WORD SYLLABLE	PRONUNCIATION
arrow	oski' naki'	os-ki' na-ki'	oh-skee' nah-kee'
bow	tanampalhlhi'	ta-nam-palh-lhi'	tah-nam-panthl-thlee'
Chickasaw	Chikasha	Chi-ka-sha	Chi-kash-shah
dance	hilha'	hi-lha'	hi-thlah'
elder	kamassa'	ka-mas-sa'	kah-mas-sah'
feather	foshi' hishi'	fo-shi' hi-shi'	foh-shi' hi-shi'
government	inaalhpisa'	i-naalh-pi-sa'	en-nathl-pee-sah'
hello	chokma	chok-ma	chog-mah
Indian Territory	Hattak Api' Homma' Iyaakni'	Hat-tak A-pi' Hom-ma' I-yaak-ni'	Ha-tak Ah-pee' Hom-mah' En-yaag-nee'
joy	ayokpa	a-yok-pa	ah-yohk-pah
Kullihoma	Kali-homma'	Ka-li-hom-ma'	Ka-lih-hom-mah'
language	anompa	a-nom-pa	ah-nom-pah
moccasins	sholosh	sho-losh	shoh-lohsh

GLOSSARY

ENGLISH WORD	CHICKASAW	WORD SYLLABLE	PRONUNCIATION
name	holhchifo	holh-chi-fo	hothl-chi-foh
Oklahoma	Oklahomma'	Ok-la-hom-ma'	Oh-gla-hom-mah'
pishofa	tashpishofa	tash-pi-sho-fa	tansh-pi-shoh-fah
quiver	oski' naki' aalhto'	os-ki' na-ki' aalh-to'	oh-skee' nah-kee' ahthl-toh'
regalia	naafokha	naa-fok-ha	nah-fohk-hah
stickball	kapochcha' to'li'	ka-poch-cha' to'-li'	kah-pohch-cha' toh'-lee'
Tishominko	Tishominko	Ti-sho-min-ko	Ti-shoh-meen-koh
unconquered	ikimambo	ik-im-am-bo	ick-im-am-boh
vegetable	nannawaa'	nann-a-waa'	nan-nah-wah'
White Dog	Ofi' Tohbi'	O-fi' Toh-bi'	Oh-fee' Toh-bee'
xylography	talhlhi	talh-lhi	tathl-thlee
yarn	nantanna' toba'	nan-tan-na' to-ba'	nahn-tahn-nah' toh-bah'
zigzag	foloto'wa	fo-lo-to'-wa	foh-loh-toh'-wah

WHAT DID YOU LEARN?

1. Identify three items used for hunting.

2. List the three branches of Chickasaw government.

3. What is the Chickasaw word for hello?

4. Describe characteristics that Tishominko or a Chickasaw warrior would have.

5. Where were the Chickasaws forced to move to in the 1830s?

6. What do Chickasaws call corn, beans, and squash?

7. What happened to the White Dog after the Chickasaw ancestors got to the Mississippi River in the great migration story?

8. Name one of the two other names for stickball.

9. What is pishofa?

10. Which direction do you dance at a stomp dance?

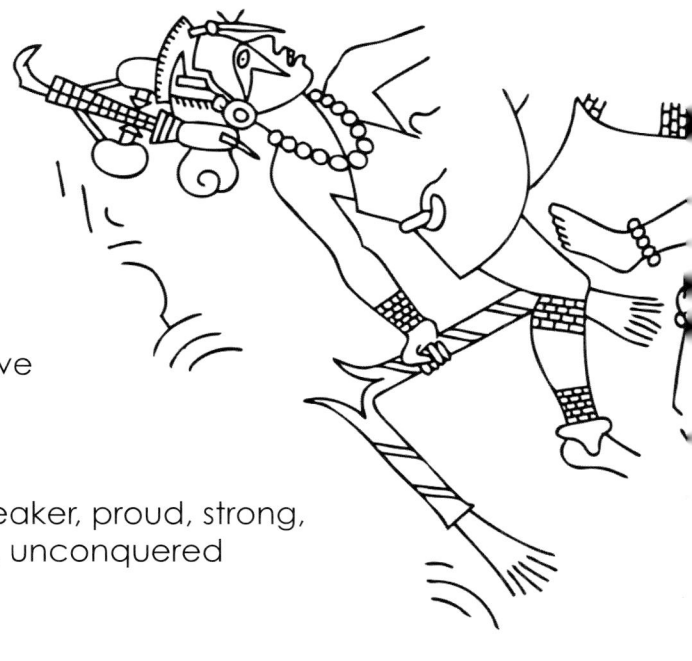

1. Arrow, bow, and quiver

2. Executive, judicial, and legislative

3. Chokma

4. Brave, honest, leader, good speaker, proud, strong, strength, intrepid, fearless, wise, unconquered

5. Indian Territory or Oklahoma

6. Three Sisters

7. The White Dog's raft came apart, and he was separated from everyone else and unable to continue the journey with the people.

8. Little Brother of War or kapochcha' to'li'

9. Traditional Chickasaw dish made of cracked corn and pork cooked on an open fire.

10. Counter-clockwise

ANSWERS

BEYOND THE ALPHABET...
ACTIVITIES AND DISCUSSION

Tishominko lived a long time ago in the seventeen and eighteen hundreds. Life was very different back then compared to life today. If he were alive today, what questions would you ask him?

Draw a map of Oklahoma and locate the Chickasaw Nation boundaries.

Write your own recipe for pishofa or for a dish that uses the Three Sisters. Make a shopping list of the ingredients you will use, and write instructions on how to prepare your dish.

Describe the game of stickball and how it might have been played hundreds of years ago.

Draw your own picture of a Chickasaw warrior. Write a description to go with your picture.

Does your family have any traditions or something that you do together every year? Write about that time with your family and why it is special.